Evolution of a Salesman:

Survival of the Fittest

I dedicate this book to my Grandpa Pete. The best man I know and who makes everyone's life he touches better.

Table of Contents

Foreword

It's always inspiring to see someone come into their full potential. Over the last few years I've had the pleasure of watching DJ go through experiences, gain expertise and exponentially grow because of it. I believe there could not have been a better person called to write this book. DJ tells this story straight from his own personal experiences.

The best part about this book is that it's for everyone. Evolutions start somewhere and DJ's journey starts at the beginning. Maybe you're just beginning as well. This book will help you become aware and avoid costly mistakes along your new path.

If you've been playing the game a while longer, you'll enjoy the later parts of this book best. That's where the newest evolutions have occurred and I'm sure it will greatly benefit you to have a glimpse of what your future (and its obstacles) look like.

You'll also find that DJ has the knowledge, and personal evolution and speaks from the heart. One of the hardest things to do is tell the world your real story and put yourself out there like that. DJ has done a great job and you're gonna love every word of this powerful sales book everyone in sales should read.

Ryan Stewman aka *Hardcore Closer*

Introduction

The principles in this book have been the key to any of my successes and will continue to be the foundation for every level of achievement that I attain in life. I guarantee that if you implement and use the same principles in your life and business, you will reach goals that you never thought were possible. You'll hit new levels of success that you've only dreamed about.

The format of this book is a little bit different than other business books that you'll read. It's in a story format, told as if you, the reader, is attending a business growth seminar. This seminar is for business owners and sales people who want to increase their sales and grow their businesses. More specifically, it's for those looking to break the glass ceiling above them.

I'm a speaker at this event and at certain points during my presentation, I will be asking different people in the audience to share about his or her business. I will take their stories and show them how applying these business principles will help them achieve new heights, and see their business in a new perspective.

These examples will show how these principles work in ANY business. Even if it isn't your industry, their stories will show how these elements can be molded to your respective business, and adapted to fit your needs. I will show you how implementing simple strategies will take your career and business to new heights.

Chapter 1

Ladies and gentleman, without further ado, DJ Christofferson.

Hello, everyone, I'm DJ and thank you for the warm introduction. I'm not a real rah, rah guy, so I won't get you on your feet and make you dance around, and I'm really not that funny, so I'm not going to tell you a joke to get you primed.

What I'm going to do is share with you my quick story and how it lead me to where I am today and how it plays into why I'm on this stage. But most importantly, I want to share with you principles that will grow your business, explode your sales, and be the catalyst *and* foundation for your future success.

Let's jump in. With the exception of my mom, who used to be a realtor, my entire family is blue collar. Union workers, tradesmen, truck drivers. Your typical blue collar family. But as long as I can remember, I wanted to be in business. Specifically, I wanted to be in sales. Even in high school, when I looked at colleges, I wanted to go someplace that actually had a sales degree and found one not too far away. I'm from Wisconsin, and currently still live there. But the school was Western Michigan University in Kalamazoo, Michigan and decided that was where I wanted to go.

Unlike most everyone else who was excited to just party, I was excited to get into the real world and work. Don't get me wrong, I partied alright but it wasn't my main focus. I wanted to graduate in four years and worked my ass off to make it happen. I wanted to start selling. While in college, I was working for a Fortune 500 company, but that sounds fancier than what it was. It was a big paint company, and I was working at one of their retail stores. The job involved retail and contractor sales. I enjoyed learning about their products, the company and how to better sell to our customers, and found that I had a pretty good knack for it. So much so contractors asked for me by name and preferred to work with me over the managers. Looking back it wasn't because I knew everything, because I didn't, but I firmly believe it was because I got to know the customers, asked them lots of questions about the projects they were working on, and always did it with a smile. Super simple yet incredibly effective, and it proved to be a building block for my sales career.

Anyway, back to school. I graduated magna cum laude, which really doesn't mean anything, and you know, if you're in sales, your degree doesn't mean a whole heck of a lot which I was soon to find that out, once I got into the real world.

Upon graduation, I got offered a job to manage a store back in Wisconsin, so I went into retail management. Let me tell you, retail management sucks. You work your tail off like you own the place but get paid crap. You have the late nights, managing knucklehead employees, always on-call in the event an employee doesn't show up, handling customer complaints, inventory. Like I said, everything an owner does but without the upside of big money. As a manager, I barely made more than thirty thousand. But I knew retail management was just the stepping stone to where I wanted to be and I worked my way up quickly to an outside sales rep position. This was around 2008 and my sales territory was focused on new residential construction.

If you're familiar with that time, that's also right about when the mortgage bubble burst, and millions of people started going through foreclosure. New construction stopped in an instant, and I found myself without a client-customer base. Many of my accounts lost tons of business or simply went out of business. So all of a sudden, my customers were gone, but I decided not to throw a pity party and instead figure out a way to continue to make business happen. So I started looking at our other products that weren't related to new residential construction, and I saw an opportunity for some niche markets.

I started doing research, and I found these niche markets bought a lot of these products. So I started looking at my territory to see if there were indeed any customers in these markets. And there were a good amount of these companies around and they did lots of business. I started learning about these products and tested them out against the competitor's products who had lion's share of the market. To my surprise our products easily held their own and in some cases were vastly superior to our competitors. So I began to walk into these businesses, ask for who was in charge of buying their products, and gave a product demo on the spot. Now, these companies weren't accustomed to this. Most sales reps that serviced these industries didn't do that. But I knew I could get them to buy if I got in front of them and buy they did. Now, the nice thing about these products is we made very nice margin on them. MUCH better margin than what we made on our core products. In fact, even though these niche products sold for a fraction of the price of our core products we made more money on each unit sold than we did on many of our core products. So even though my overall sales were down, I was able to double the profit of my territory versus the previous sales rep who covered the territory. Sales were down but profits were up.

I continued forward with this strategy and go after new contracts. One that I was working on for a while was huge. I can't even tell you how much business they did. I wasn't smart enough at that time to look and see how much they did. I just knew that they did business all across the country. They had tons of vehicles and huge buildings. I knew that they did a lot. They would buy products, pallets at a time. I got in with them and I was starting to make some headway into their company. Then one day, I got a call into the district manager's office and was told that my territory was being downsized. They told me that I could go back into retail management, but I never want to go backwards. Only forward. The worst part was that this huge contract I had worked hard to get was given to another sales rep. The dude even bragged to me about the appointment he was going to meet them. Obviously, that really pissed me off. I was getting the shaft here because I was the "newest" rep yet was the only one who'd had the balls to go after these new accounts.

That was my first taste of the sales industry and working for a big company. I realized then and there that a company that values seniority over profitability was something I would never go back to. No, I knew I had to do something else.

Chapter 2

I mulled over the offer to go back into retail sales and retail management for less than a minute. Actually, I wanted to tell my district manager to kiss something but I refrained. At this time I was still in my young 20s and thought I'd have zero issues finding a job. I told myself, "I graduated magna cum laude. I've got all these great credentials. It'll be easy for me to find a job. Who wouldn't hire a young 20-something that is aggressive, and willing to go after it?" So I put my résumés out there thinking I'd have a new career in a week. Only the calls never came. Let me correct that. The only calls I got were from multi-level marketing companies which wasn't for me. To say that I was shocked and embarrassed was an understatement.

After not finding a new job for a while, my mother approached me. She was a real estate agent at that time and asked me if I wanted to get into real estate sales. I told her no. I had basically lost a job because there was no real estate business happening. There was no new construction. People weren't buying houses. People weren't selling houses. The economy sucked. Why would I go into real estate? Well after another month of not being able to get a job, real estate started looking attractive and I decided I was going to give it a shot. I studied my butt off and got my license about a week or two later. I was now a real estate agent. Thankfully I had my mom, because she helped me get started with some people that she knew. Without my mom, there's probably no way I would have made it into the real estate world as quickly as I did.

Now what I'm going to share next is important to know, because it helped build my philosophy on how I was going to build my business. So, I'm working with my very first two buyers that I was able to get on my own, and I referred them to the in-office lender at my company. It was an awful experience. Actually, that doesn't do justice on how bad it was. My buyers had zero idea what was going on ever. They had no idea if their loan was going to happen. There was no communication from the lender. They would leave voicemails with the lender, and then get an email at 11:30 at night if they were lucky. The lender wouldn't respond to me and hid from the office so I couldn't talk to her. It was terrible. The closings were late. Even at the closing table, we still didn't know if the closing was going to happen on both of these. You can imagine, as a new realtor, I needed these deals. My buyers were first-time home buyers. They were freaking out, and looking to me for reassurance, and I had no idea what to do. I had to go to the lender's boss, and to find out what was going on and that clown then hid from me! The silver lining though was those experiences shaped my outlook on how client interaction should go. I also realized that if I refer my buyers to a lender, and that lender does a terrible job, I'm obviously not going to get referrals from my clients, because they're going to be pissed at me for making that recommendation. Heck, I was pissed at me for recommending that lender.

As a couple more months passed I started to hit my stride in real estate. Business was good and I was a rising star. But at the same time I realized that selling homes wasn't for me. I didn't really like it. Obviously, now as a lender, I work with a lot of Realtors every single day. I'm not bashing the field or anything like that, but it just wasn't for me. That begs the question, "How did I get started in lending?" As my real estate business started heating up I started sending my buyers to a certain mortgage company which happens to be the same company I work for now. I really liked the service they provided, and I liked the people there. To top things off I became close friends with the president of the company. He doesn't have any sons, so maybe I became a little like a surrogate son to him. We were having breakfast one morning, talking about business, goals and such, and he asked me how real estate was going and if I liked it. I told him the truth. I didn't really like it. It wasn't for me, I didn't like the hours, didn't like showing houses, and I'm not that sentimental of a guy to deal with sellers who thought their homes were worth more than they really were. He then asked me, point blank, if I had ever thought about being a lender.

The truth of the matter was, I had thought about it. Because of the awful experiences I had at the beginning of my real estate career, I knew that I could do it better. At that breakfast, in this place in a town called Delafield, my mortgage career began.

Chapter 3

So I quit the real estate world, and entered the mortgage world. All my Realtor friends thought I was a traitor by going to the lender's side of the table. All the lenders thought that I was an idiot for ever being a Realtor. I quickly realized that there was a lot of animosity between lenders and Realtors. I already knew from the Realtor's side of the table that a lot of them don't like lenders. When I went to the lender side of the table, I realized a lot of lenders didn't like Realtors. To me, it never made sense to have that divide, because both have the same client and the same goal; to close as soon as possible and as smoothly as possible. Otherwise, nobody gets paid.

When I went into the lender world, I knew that I had two different types of clients. This is very normal, and it should be normal to a lot of lenders. However, lenders in general don't have this mindset. The first client a lender has represents a B2B relationship. That's the relationship between you and the Realtor or your other referral sources. Then you have the B2C relationship. This is the business to consumer relationship, or in the case with lending, it would be to the borrower, whether the consumer is buying a house or refinancing one. You need to treat these two relationships differently. You need to treat them well and work to build those relationships in order to grow your business.

It seemed so elementary, but I noticed that most lenders really focused all of their efforts onto the borrower. They had no interest in talking with the Realtors. To me, it's stupid. I knew that I wanted to build my business in a way that catered both to the borrowers and to the Realtors. I knew if I did a good job with the borrowers, I would then get more referrals from them. Referrals are great. Also, I knew if I did a great job with the Realtors, I would get more of their business and more of their referrals. The question is, how do you do that? How did I do that?

You might not be a lender or a Realtor, but the principle I want to share with you is going to be applicable to everybody, not matter what you sell. This is the foundation of how you build any business, whether you're selling a product, or selling a service. You need to bring massive value to your client, whether that's a referral source, or an actual consumer who purchases your service and/or your product. It's all about bringing them massive value.

We're going to get more in depth into that in a little bit, but I'm going to continue on with my story. As a lender I asked myself, "What kind of value can I bring to my real estate agents? Was I going to focus more on B2B relationships or this stuff?" What do Realtors want? I was a former Realtor and had an idea of what they wanted and it was pretty simple. They want to have great communication. That can mean something slightly different for every Realtor but mostly they want to be updated with everything. They want to have their process and transactions to go smoothly. There are parts to a real estate deal. There's the loan commitment, which basically means that the loan has been processed and has been underwritten already. It means the loan has been conditionally approved, prior to the closing day. Agents also want closing to happen on time, by the set date in the contract. If you don't close on time, it's bad for the client, because there are people moving and they have moving vans ready, and people ready to help them move. A lot of times, the seller needs the proceeds from closing on their former home to buy a new house. If you don't hit your closing date on time, it's a big mess for the buyer and the seller. It also means the Realtor doesn't get their commission check on time.

I started building my business based on these three simple principles: Great communication; hit my loan commitments on time, every time; and hit my closing dates on time, every time. I know it's not anything earth-shattering, but it worked well. It worked very well. My first year in the business of being a lender, I shattered all of our company's rookie records even though we were in a very down economy and more difficult lending environment. I did whatever I had to do to meet those three things. As I built my business, I focused and hammered those three things. My business grew, then I doubled the next year. I grew my business again the following year. Then I hit a plateau.

I hit a glass ceiling, which is where I feel a lot of people may be in this room. You're making a certain amount of money, and do every year, year in and year out, but you want to take it to the next level. You know that you have the ability to take it to the next level, but something there is blocking you. That's what was happening to me. I took those three principles and made it as big as I could, and did as well as I could before I hit that ceiling.

I want to share with you what helped me break that glass ceiling. Because I learned this principle, there is no longer a ceiling above my head.

Chapter 4

The principle I'm talking about is bringing massive value. I mentioned it before. I have learned that the value you bring will only take you to certain heights. Three principles; great communication, on-time loan commitments and on-time closings, had made me a lot of money. However, I found that I was capped out for three years in a row, and made almost the exact same amount of money. I decided, "I need to find something. I need to do something for my real estate agents that will bring them more value. I need something that's going to help them grow their business." That was the key. I had to do more than just make their business easier by communicating and closing the loans on time. I had to help them grow. But how could I help them grow their business?

There was this thing, the Internet, which had been around for a long time. Believe it or not, I was not a big proponent of using the

Internet. I didn't even have a Facebook account for a while. Finally, I got on Facebook, thinking that there's got to be something I can do with it. I didn't even know about Facebook marketing or anything like that. I started looking online and researching, "How can I grow business for real estate using Facebook and using the Internet? I'm going to learn this stuff. I'm going to teach it to Realtors." I'm a young guy and the average age of lenders and Realtors is 50-something. Generally speaking, they're not too tech savvy. I figured out, "This is stuff I can learn. I can teach them how to use it for their business, and I can help them grow."

I started searching and I came across this rambunctious, crazy guy that cost a lot, swore a lot, had tattoos and all these things. I started watching his videos, and it began to make sense to me. He was talking about how to use Facebook, how to use videos, how to use all these different things to grow your business. I thought, "OK, I could take this and learn it and apply just for myself. Or I could take this information, learn it, and I can help Realtors implement it in their business." I knew if I used these tools only for myself, I could only grow so much, because I'm just one person. But if I could teach 10 realtors these ideas, help them grow their business and make them happy, then business will come to me and I would be able to grow exponentially." I watched his videos. I signed up for one of his courses. I actually flew down to Texas and did a live workshop, and started learning this stuff. I spent the next year of my life learning these ideas. At the same time, I was still practicing my three basic principles. I spent countless hours and tens of thousands of dollars learning this Facebook stuff, Internet marketing, all these different things to become as much of an expert as I could possibly be on social media marketing.

I'm still far from where I can and will be as time goes, but I found out that I was light years ahead of everybody else in the lending industry and in the real estate industry. I started teaching workshops. Realtors would come into my office and I would teach them. I didn't charge them any money. If you know Realtors, a lot of them will go to things if there's free food or free stuff and the commitment is a little bit low. The same thing is true with lenders. But I made my workshops the opposite of that. I told them there would be no food. I told them, "You have to be there every single week. It's two hours straight. You have to show up on time." I was very vigilant. I was very disciplined in that because if you didn't learn part one, part two would not make sense. You need part one to learn part two, and you need to learn part two to learn part three.

The way I presented was to tell them I could help them grow their business, versus just saying, "Hey, I'm this lender. Let's get lunch, and then I will tell you about this new stupid program." It was, "Hey, I'm this lender. Unlike other lenders who only take your business, I want to help you grow your business, to show you how you will close one to two extra deals per month." If you are a Realtor, what sounds better? A lender saying, "I'm helping you to grow your business by closing one or two deals a month." Or, "Hey, I'm a lender. Let me show you this new program I have." Obviously, it's the first one, and that's what I did. That's what I have been using to grow my business, and to take it to the next heights. I'm providing massive value and that has grown into other avenues and other opportunities that I didn't even consider, like speaking here to you today. And it's all because my focus is bringing massive value to my relationships which is what we're going to talk about next.

Chapter 5

We all have natural abilities and talents, but those things can only take us so far. However, we aren't capped by our natural abilities and talents. We all have inside of us the ability to go to new heights, new levels, and make more money than we ever dreamed possible. It's not because you're special. None of us is special. We might have some gifts that are above other people, but we also know people who waste those gifts. We all know a lot of very talented losers in our lives, people who had all of the ability, but it amounted to nothing. We also all know the people that had nothing growing up and had a hellish life, yet they became super successful.

As an example, look at my career. We'll just use income, because that's what people tend to look at when measuring success. I'm from Wisconsin, so the incomes go a lot further there than some other places. My natural abilities took me to about six figures, which is nothing to complain about. Most people are very happy with a six figure income. But I knew I could do more. The thing is, most people stop at that. They get to that magic number. But know, six figures today doesn't go nearly as far as it did 20 years ago. I knew I could do more, but I was capped.

When I began to bring value to my clients, both to my Realtors and to the consumers, my borrowers, I begin to see my income grow. I saw it go from six figures to a multiple six-figure income, which again, is a very high income. That income made me one of the top couple percent in the country and the entire world, but I knew I could do more. The problem was, I kept hitting that plateau where I made the same income, year in and year out, for three years. I knew that I had to do something differently to grow my business, and that involved bringing new value into my relationships with my Realtors.

Now, I'm going to be open with you and it's not bragging or anything like that. It's to put into perspective how powerful this is. In the next 18 months, I will make seven figures. Then 18 months from then it'll be multiple seven figures. Why? It's because now I know that whenever I hit the glass ceiling, all I have to do is add another level of value to my relationships. This is possible for you as well even if you don't think so. How is it possible? Because you'll discover that as you hit each new level, you'll find new opportunities. You'll make new connections that are going expand your mind and business in ways that you never knew possible.

If you had asked me a few years ago if I'd be speaking at this seminar, I would've said, "Heck no." This opportunity arose because of the value that I've brought to my clients, and as a result of that value, people have taken notice from across the country and wanted to know more. And as this opportunity arose, other opportunities came to me. Just recently, I was invited to be in a high-end, worldwide Mastermind, where people are making multiple seven figures per year. In that group I'm a peon! But you can see how I *know* that my income will continue growing because of the added value I'll learn in this mastermind and be able to implement into my businesses.

These opportunities came to me because I brought value. A very simple concept that is often thought about but rarely put into practice because people care about themselves too much and not enough about their clients and referral sources. Now, let's go more into the theory of the evolution of a salesman. As we go into that, I want you to picture yourself in there, and see where you are inside that life cycle.

Chapter 6

We have all heard of the Theory of Evolution and the concept of survival of the fittest. But let's quickly recap the Theory of Evolution. Basically, the theory is that all life started from a very basic, single celled organism, which over time, grew into something bigger and stronger over millions and billions of years. For instance, take humans. In this theory, we started off as a single celled organism, which over millions of years became primates and then over the course of millions of more years, we evolved into humans. Now, you may or may not believe in this theory. I am one who doesn't. However, we can still take this concept and apply it to our careers, especially the part of the theory, Survival of the Fittest. Basically Survival of the Fittest occurs when species compete to survive and adapt to their surroundings. The "fittest" survive, while the weak die off and become extinct. There are different animals that died off through the course of time because they could not keep up with the environmental changes. That's why they call it survival of the fittest.

The same thing goes on in the business world. There is a survival of the fittest. You see people in their careers that go from job to job. They get to a certain level and burn-out, or they can never achieve a certain income level, or they can never break through their glass ceiling. They blame it on external circumstances. "I didn't have this report." "Oh, this product's no good." "Our price is terrible." "I can't do this," or "I can't do that." That's because they're not built to survive. They are not able to evolve with the changes in the economy, market, buyers, and consumers. Things change rapidly, and in this technological age that we are in, things are changing faster than ever before. When it comes to business, if you want to evolve as time goes, you have to continually evolve and add to the value that you bring to your clients, whether they are your referral sources and/or customers.

When it comes to survival of the fittest you have to ask yourself, "Am I growing? Am I adapting, or am I going to be axed out? Am I going to go extinct?" A lot of people in my field, the lending world, are afraid of being taken over by the Internet. For instance, there are countless commercials that tout an automated mortgage processes, which makes it so simple that it gets rid of the loan officer. I hear loan officers complaining about this all of the time, but I have no fear of that. Why? Because I will continue to bring value to a customer and a Realtor that no computer program can ever produce. I'll always stay ahead of the game in that regard. Let me give you an example.

I know Realtors that were incredibly successful. However, the real estate industry has changed dramatically over the last few years, and as a result they're making less and less money each and every year. It's because they have continued to rely on technology that people aren't using much anymore, such as home phones. Maybe they're still doing well from an income standpoint in most people's eyes, but they are doing nowhere near what they could be doing if they adapted with the times. Instead of their businesses being cut in half, they could be growing their business if they were willing to change and grow as their environment changes.

What is this idea of bringing value? That's what I want to talk about it. You may have heard it before. You may be thinking, "Well, this doesn't sound like anything new. This sounds like things I may have heard before." You're right; I didn't invent this. I didn't make it up. I didn't even discover it. It's stuff that's been around before I was born, before you were born, and even before the medieval times. This principle has been around for thousands and thousands of years. Which is what we're talking about next.

Chapter 7

My favorite book is the Bible. I'm a Christian and I'm not afraid to talk about that. That's who I am. Now, there's a principle in the Bible that many people repackage and give it a new name, but it originated in the Bible. "You reap what you sow." Reaping what you sow is pretty simple. Say you're a farmer, and you're planting tomato seeds. What are you going to reap? Are going to reap cucumbers? No, you're going to grow tomatoes. Super simple, right? It's the same principle with anything in life. If you want to make more money, you need to sow in other people's lives, bring in value, and help their lives become better.

The referral part is to help them grow their business, make their lives easier and get them more sales. As you plug into them, you benefit their business, and in turn, you will reap a benefit for yourself. It's very simple. Zig Ziglar says, "You can have everything in life you want, if you will just help other people get what they want." It's the same principle. You reap what you sow. If you pour into other people, you will get a benefit in return. However, you can't do it from a selfish perspective, only concerned about yourself. You have to do it from an empathetic heart.

Jay Abraham, talks about the Strategy of Preeminence. In some of his interviews, he talks about how he is different when he talks to people because he genuinely cares about his clients and their success. He doesn't just give them frosting-covered talks. He really talks to them because he wants to help them grow. He shows that he cares, and demonstrates empathy to them. He steps inside their shoes to help them. As they are more successful, Jay is more successful. It's brilliant. If you ever get a chance, listen to his stuff. It'll blow you away. He probably explains it way better than I ever will, but it's the same principle. You reap what you sow!

Sow into people's lives. If you help them achieve everything that they want, you and your business will grow. I know it sounds really simple, and it really is that simple. The difficult part, which isn't very difficult at all, is to figure out, what do you do bring that value? What do you sow? What are the different things that you can bring into a person's business? That's where your referral partners and clients come in. How can you help bring massive value to them, so that they are more successful? Instead of telling you, or giving you a mathematical formula, which there isn't one, I want to do something a bit more fun and interactive. I want to call some people up from the audience and talk about their business. And using the principle of reaping and sowing, I want to demonstrate how to bring massive value into their business for their clients. In return, they will reap financial gains.

Chapter 8

The way this is going to work, we'll have the ushers coming up and down the aisle. If you have a business card, I want you to put your business card into the baskets that we pass around. If you don't have a business card, write your name on a piece of scrap paper. I'm going to pick randomly a few different people. I'll do three to five of them, depending on time. I'm going to ask you a few different things. If you're afraid to stand up and talk in front of people, or afraid to talk about your business, do not put your card or your scrap paper into the basket, because I'm going to be asking you some questions.

I'm not going to be coming at you. I genuinely want to bring you value, and try to help you grow your business. Why? Because I know if you're more successful, even from our little relationship here, I will be more successful as well. I genuinely care about your business, and want to provide more value to you, value that you could pass on to your clients. I'll be asking questions like: What's your name? What's your business? What do you do? What is your unique selling position? What do you do better than the competition? How do you sell your products and your service? I'm also going to ask you, where do you cap out and what are your struggles? From there, I'm going to just throw out some ideas, off the cuff, of things that you can do in your business, beginning tomorrow, to at least start putting the pieces together. These are ideas that will catapult you to the next level of success in your business. Once you take that piece of advice, and plant those seeds that I'm going to give you, you're going to hit a new level. When you hit that new level of success, when you feel like you can't go further, you can still go further. You just have to find new opportunities, or new ways to bring value into the equation.

All right, there's a couple hundred of you here, so I'm going to give everybody another minute or two to put in your business card or scrap paper. This is the most important part of everything that we're going to be talking about today. You may not have understood all that I've said with the flow of my words, as I stumble, mumble and bumble, but one of the things I want to do is bring real value and show you how we can implement these principles. Everything is about implementation. If you can go away with even one small thing that you can implement into your business, you will reap 10 fold, 50 fold, 100 fold, even 1,000 fold.

Chapter 9

All, right, let's pick a person out of the basket. First person is John Phillips. John, can you stand up for everybody, please. I'm sure you can see John in the back. Ushers, please bring a microphone over to him. Thank you very much. John, how's it going today?

It's going great, DJ.

I'm glad to hear, John. May I ask you a question? What do you do for a living?

I'm a real estate agent.

Real estate agent? Wonderful. I'm glad I got an easy one. Right in my wheelhouse, to start things off. You're a real estate agent. How long have you been selling real estate?

Well, DJ, I've been doing this for about 20 years.

All right, John, have you been doing it full-time for 20 years?

Well, no, but about the last 15 years I've been at it full-time. I started off for five years part-time, helping family and friends, eventually started doing enough where I tried to give it a go. I've been doing it ever since.

John, that's wonderful to hear. Also, I'm glad to hear that you've made it through the tough times, with the recent lean years, was it 2008, '09, and '10? May I ask you, how did you make it through that, when so many other Realtors decided to give up their license, go out and find different jobs?

I'm not going to lie, it was pretty difficult, and I did think about quitting. Business got really, really slow, but thankfully, I had a good base, referrals who sent me enough where I could squeak by. I'm still standing.

That's right, John. You're still standing, and what I want to do today is hopefully provide you some knowledge, some value to bring into your business, for your business to bring to your clients, so that when the next downturn in the economy happens, that you won't be losing market share. Your business will not drop, and it actually will grow. Whenever there's a downturn in the economy, there are a few sets of people that will make it extra big. The piece of the pie is smaller, because the economy is down. But what happens is that a lot of people drop out of the industry, so there's fewer mouths trying to get that pie. The value that I want to drop on you today is going to help you grow your business now, and even help it explode your business when the market is down. Does that sound good to you?

That sounds awesome, DJ. I would love any kind of help that I can get, or anything you can provide me.

That's exactly what I'm here to do. Let me ask you, you have buyers and sellers, which clients do you want to talk about today? Who do you want to grow? Which one of those two do you want to grow?

I'd like to grow both, obviously, but if I had to pick one, let's talk about sellers and listings. Listings, let's talk about listings.

How many listings did you sell last year?

I just did my numbers recently, and I had 27 closings that were listings last year.

Twenty-seven, that's a very good number, a strong number. What percent of your houses expired, would you say?

I have a 90% sale rate, so 10% expired.

10%, so that means, if my math is correct, you had 30 houses that you listed. Three of them expired, and so you sold 27?

That would be right, DJ.

John, how many listings do you want to sell? Not list, but sell, next year?

I'd like to sell 50 houses.

You'd like to sell 50 houses, and to do that, there are two different ways. One is you could sell more of your listings. For you, though, if you sold 100% of the same number that you have now, the most you could do would be 30. That's not going to get you to your 50. The next thing you can look at, is you can close more, and get more listings from your listing appointments. Let me ask you, of the listing appointments you go on, what percent of those do you get hired?

That's, really, only about 50 percent. Every 10 I go on, I'd say about 5.

You get 50 percent, now. Out of the 50 percent that you get, are those mostly from referrals or marketing? Where are you getting those?

Most of them, actually, are from the referrals. I don't do too well on the listing appointments I get from different marketing things that I do.

OK, John, so tell me, you close 50%, you had 30 listings. That means you went on 60 listing appointments, and you got 30 of those listings, and closed 27. You can see right there, you have a huge window of opportunity already to get more of those 60. The way you do that is you've got to bring value to them. What are the two things that all sellers want most? What are the two things they want from their listing agent? What's the outcome they want? It's simple. They want to sell their house quickly, and they want to sell it for the most amount of money. John, how does a Realtor go about selling the house quickly, and for the most amount of money?

There's a lot of things that go on. You have to list it right, you have to have good pictures, you have to have the house on the Internet, the MLS system, and all these different sites. That's basically what you need in a nutshell.

John, you're telling me you need to have good pictures, you need to put the house on the MLS, and you need to have pricing right. Is that right?

Yeah, that's right.

Now, that sounds pretty easy, doesn't it? When you break that down in simple terms, it doesn't sound too difficult to do. You hire a professional photographer for $100, $200, whatever it costs, and get good pictures. Find out about the houses around your house that have sold, and list it at the right price. Spend $500 on a flat-fee MLS, to get the house on the Internet, right? Now, I'm not bashing. Just hear me out, here. That sounds pretty basic, with very little value added, because anybody can do that.

For a $500 MLS flat service, they can do all that for themselves. If you want to close more of those appointments you go on, you need to separate your marketing plan from the competition. When I see people in the real estate profession, specifically, they all have the very same basic marketing plan. I'm going to take pictures, I'm going to put a sign in the yard, I'm going to send out some just listed cards, and then I'll get the house on the MLS, so, it will be on all the big websites. Let me tell you, though, they're not separating themselves from the others. Why? Because, we already talked about it. You can get that same service from the flat service brokers. I know people will say, what about contract negotiation? What about answering phone calls? What about this, and that? Yes, those are all important, but, you agree that the two most important things to a seller are selling the house for top dollar, and selling their house as quickly as possible. This is true for most people. How do you do that? You need to have a marketing plan that accentuates those two pressure points, those two pain points, for a seller. You need to be able to go to them, and say, "I know everybody else does this. I know everybody else puts a sign in their yard. I know everybody else takes some pictures. I know everybody else here puts the house on the MLS, and goes all to the big sites, but with my marketing plan, we do that, plus more. The main focus of my marketing plan is to get your house in front of the right people, the people most apt to purchase your house. Everybody else just throws it on the Internet. It's kind of like they just take spaghetti, throw it against the wall, and see what sticks. That's not the way I do my marketing, because that way is inefficient. If you want to sell your house fast, you've got to get your house in front of the right people, the people who can afford your house. You also have to do that at the right time. These are people that are most likely to purchase your house. My marketing plan is very specific to the person and the demographic that would purchase your house. Let me ask you, Mr. and Mrs.

Seller, what do you think would be more effective? A marketing plan that just goes to the masses, and hopes something sticks, or a marketing plan that is specifically targeted to the people most interested in purchasing your house? Obviously, the one that's most specifically targeted to the demographics. My marketing plan does that. Which house is going to sell quicker? The one that's broader or the one that's more narrow-focused, like mine? The one that's more narrow-focused, of course. Which one's going to get top-dollar? It's obviously going to be mine, too. Do you know why? It's because when I am marketing to the people most apt to purchase your house, more of the right people are going to start bidding against each other. There are going to be more people, and more, better quality showings. When you target to the right people, they are going to create a bidding war for your home." John, that all sounds great, doesn't it? If you went on 10 listing appointments, how many of those listings do you think that you would get, if you were to present a value equation for them, or a marketing plan that hits their pain points to sell their house?

You'd pretty much get damn near all of them. The ones that you won't get are the ones that are probably just interviewing with you because they have to do it. They feel that they have to do it and they're just going to go with their friend, regardless.

I don't care what real estate agent you're going up against, even if it's the one that says they've sold a hundred million dollars of homes in the last year. It's pretty easy to sell hundreds of million dollars of homes, when all you do is beat down the price and sell below market value. I know those Realtors that do that, but you're not. You're going to sell them at their pain points. You're going to bring value to them. You need a marketing plan that's going to help you do that.

DJ, that all sounds good. I would love to learn how I do that. I don't know what that marketing plan looks like.

John, I'm glad you asked, because that's what I'm here to do, as well. Not just for you, John. I know some of you, in the audience, are going to want some help implementing the plans that we're going to talk about, into your business. As part of the value that I'm going to be bringing in, I'm starting a program. It's not exactly coaching or consulting. I don't really have a name for it. But, I'm going to work with the people who sign up for my brand new program, to implement a value strategy into their business and to help take them to the next level. That's what I'm going to do, so stayed tuned for that. John, if you're interested in that, make sure you stayed tuned. I'm going to tell you how to get set-up for that, and how you can interview for that position, because I won't take everybody.

I want to work with people that are determined, motivated, and, obviously, that are going to do the work. John, do you find that helpful? So, you bring value like that into your listing presentation, and address the two pain points of a seller, the outcomes they desire, by laying out a specific marketing plan. Through that plan made specifically for them, you'll easily increase your closing percentage on listing appointments. Do you see how that would work? And even better, those people will know other people who are selling. They will tell others, "You need to talk to John. This is what he did for us. His marketing plan is better than everybody's, hands-down."

Let's say you start doing your farming, and you send out your postcards every month. Instead of a postcard that says "free market analysis," you could say something like, "See the marketing plan that will get you top dollar on your house, and will sell quicker than anybody else, guaranteed."

There's some other things that I will show you, if you join the program, about how to dominate your real estate place. Was that helpful, John?

Yeah, that was awesome. Thank you so much!

My pleasure, John.

Chapter 10

Next, we got, says here, Michelle. Oh, crap. It's one of these [laughs] Polish names. Michelle Kapinski. Yeah, right there in the front row. Usher, can you bring a microphone? Michelle, did I get that right?

Yeah, DJ. [laughs] That was right. One of the first people that got it right on first try!

Well, I'm glad I could at least do that. Michelle, it says here that you are the owner, of an expedited freight company. What is expedited freight? Can you share with me what that is?

Sure. The shortest way, or simplest way to explain is that you have big companies like FedEx, and UPS, and DHL. They do things on a big national level, where you have a package that needs to go from, say, New York to Los Angeles. It's kind of like that, but it's on a smaller, local level. Let's say you have a company, and you have several branches around the area, and you need to get a package from location A to location B. We will do that.

Or let's say you need to make a local delivery for your company, to deliver your product, and you want it on the same day. It's quicker to have us do it, expedited freight, than it would be to hire UPS or FedEx. We can do it much quicker than them. Because we're local, obviously, and we have the flexibility that one of those companies won't have.

That's pretty cool, Michelle. I've never really heard of that. Is that a big thing?

Yeah. It's huge. I have probably about a hundred drivers that do this for my company. They're basically subcontractors. They work underneath me. We help get the contracts from the different companies, and we just keep those guys going, and delivering from place to place. We do it for a lot of companies in our area. Since we have over a hundred drivers, you can imagine how much we do deliver.

Let me ask you a couple of questions, so I make sure I can understand a little bit more about your business, Michelle. You're delivering these packages, whether they're delivering products that somebody bought locally, or delivering something from one company's office location to another office location in the same area. What are your clients looking for most, when it comes to expedited freight?

For the most part, it's just time. That means getting their package to them on time, whatever delivery time they set. Say they need to have it there by 5:00. It's a deadline. They need to have it there by 5:00.

Let me understand, Michelle. The biggest thing with expedited freight, expedited delivery, is the time thing? Is there a cost concern on there, where these customers are? Or is it really about just on time delivery?

Obviously, cost is somewhat of a concern, but the biggest thing for them is on-time delivery.

Michelle, let me ask you, then, do you know what your on time delivery rate is? You have a couple hundred or so drivers. I'm assuming you're doing thousands of deliveries all the time. Do you know what percent that you are getting these deliveries on time?

We're at 98% on-time delivery.

Ninety-eight percent, that's pretty awesome. That's damn near perfect. You have a 98% on-time delivery. You're saying that there's not a ton of competition out there. What are you struggling with? What are you here for, at this seminar? Sounds like things are going well. Is there a particular struggle in your business? What's shakin'?

To be honest, we seem to have plateaued, like what you were saying earlier. We have our hundred-plus drivers, and we're pretty much stuck there, because we have the same flow of customers. But we would like to grow bigger, do more business. We know we can do it. We're just hitting that glass ceiling, like you said, and not sure how to go from 100 drivers to 200 drivers.

I get it, Michelle. You want to grow your business. Are you looking to stay locally? Is there enough business for you to grow locally? I know you said there wasn't a lot of competition, but is there still business to be had in your marketplace?

Certainly, there is. That's what we would like to do first, get more market share. We probably have about 50% of the market share. However, the other 50% is broken up between five or six other companies.

That's actually a significant amount of room, Michelle, that you guys can grow. Let me ask, how are you guys going about trying to get that business from those other companies?

We have sales reps. They call on these other business, that are similar to the businesses that we work with, and try to get a shot at their business. I tell you, that's where we've struggled, not being able to get our foot in the door with other companies. We're churning through sales people.

Michelle, how are your sales reps? What are they doing on the phone, trying to get this business? What are they saying to get their foot in the door?

It really goes that we call up and let them know who we are. Everybody knows who we are, that we're the largest out there, and that we deliver on time, most of the time, most every single time. But it stops from there.

Michelle, you have all of the pieces. You have what you need to get these clients already. You just need to re-tweak. You have to repackage and reimage what you have to bring more value to those particular clients that you don't have already.

You said that you have a 98% on-time delivery rating. That's awesome. That's pretty impeccable, and that's something that you could hang in your hat on. I would assume that your sales reps are already talking about that you have a 98% on-time guaranteed delivery, right?

Yeah, of course they're mentioning those things.

Why aren't they going with you? What are they telling you?

They're happy with who they have. They say things are going pretty good there. So we

just follow up every once in a while and
hopefully that will get the business.

Michelle, that's one of mistakes your team is making. You need to be Johnny-on-the-spot. You need to be in front of these people all the time. Let me give you something that I think you could use right now to start getting the business from most people, even on these first or second sales calls. You have a 98% delivery rating. It's something that you believe, and your team delivers on time, right? Almost every time, right? That's great value.

What fear does a company have about switching? That you're going to drop the ball. That they might be that two percent that fails, right? How about you do something, which can almost eliminate that concern for that client? Obviously, there are things that can happen, blow out a tire or something like that, where you can't make your delivery. But what if you tell them something like this, "We have a 98% on-time delivery rate. What if I can guarantee for you, for all of our new clients that we're bringing onboard, we have 1000% money-back guarantee? That means that we believe so much in our service, in our on-time delivery rate, that if we were to not deliver your goods on time, we would refund you 1000% of what the delivery cost would be."

Say their delivery cost is $50. That's what your company charged them. If the delivery is late, you'd have to pay them back $500. I know that sounds like a lot, but would you risk $500 to get yourself a new client for life? How much is that one client to you, if you have that one new client for the rest of your career? Thousands upon thousands upon thousands, right? What you can do there is give this value proposition to them and say, "We believe so much in our service that we're going to put a 1000% guarantee on it." You already told me you have a 98% on-time delivery rate, so what's the fear? Yeah, you might drop the ball here and there. But the opportunity you're going to get from these other clients, the new business that you will get, is going to far offset the losses that you would have if you have to pay up the guarantee.

If you do make a mistake and you don't deliver on time, and you do have to pay 1000% back to the client, let me ask you, are they going to be pretty impressed that you actually are a company of their word? That you don't shy away from your promises, and you pay them back 1000%? Heck, yeah they will!

Start trying to do that tomorrow. Talk to your sales reps. Have a meeting and implement that strategy. I bet you that you go from 50% market share in six months' time to another 25%, because I guarantee nobody in your competition has that much faith in their service, that they're willing to put a 1000% money back guarantee.

Let me ask you, Michelle. Is that helpful? Is that going to bring a value to your business? Is that going to bring value to your clients? Are they going to have more comfort and security?

Yes, they will!

Are you going to make more money as a result of that one small little tweak into your business, that one bit of added value?

Definitely. I can't believe I never thought of that before!

Again, I'm going to say this to everyone. I know some people here want to have hands-on help. Even though the business we talk about today may differ from yours, we can take these concepts and work them into any industry. I want to help you, and after this talk, I'm going to give you some directions on how to apply for my upcoming Mastermind.

Who's next?

Chapter 11

Next we have Julie, looks like Riemer. Julie, where are you? Usher, can you please go over and hand her the microphone? Julie, how are you doing today?

I'm doing great DJ, and that's actually Reimer.

Oh, Reimer. OK. Sorry. Actually, I have friends that spell it the exact same way. One calls it Reimer, one calls it Riemer. 50 percent chance and I got it wrong. Sorry about that Julie.

Yeah, no worries.

Julie, what do you do for a living? What are you here for?

I have a small insurance brokerage, and we carry lots of different companies that we can sell insurance for. I'm really struggling with holding onto clients longer and really keeping that renewal base going. I get the initial policies, and then it seems like after a year, maybe two years, the clients leave for something cheaper. I can't seem to keep the renewals going. As you know in the insurance industry, we don't make a lot on the initial sale. It's the renewals where we make money, where you have that big base. I'm having difficulty keeping those people.

That's actually a really good one. I want to talk about that with you, Julie. Let me tell you some things that come to mind. I see this a lot in different industries and the statistics, although I don't have them off the top of my head, are staggering. We know that it's cheaper to sell to current clients than it is to sell to new, cold clients. That's the leaky bucket theory. We have a bucket with a bunch of holes in it. We keep trying to pour new customers, water, into the bucket, but the water keeps draining out. We keep putting all our effort into putting more water into the bucket, but we don't put any effort into plugging up the holes which would help us keep the current customers that we have.

From what I understand, what you're telling me is that through whatever way you do your marketing, you get people in the door. You got a good initial quote for them, let's say homeowners' policy, autos, whatever it is. Then, as time goes, whether it's a year or two, they find a different quote and switch to another company.

How are they getting different quotes and such, Julie?

Really, it's the commercials and I hear that people go to Geico.com or they go to Esurance. They see this commercial that says they could save a bunch of money. Then, they go to these sites, see it, and they switch and change over for $100 savings or $200 savings over the year.

That makes sense. Let me say something to you. I know I can speak of this from what other lenders I've talked to have told me. The same things happened to our industry. The world is trying to turn your business into a commodity, something that they can get from anywhere. The same thing is true with lenders. In order to keep yourself going, you have to differentiate yourself. You have to provide, again, value to the client that they can't get anywhere else. Insurance is a great opportunity to provide value to a client. One reason is because people know nothing about insurance. They know that they need to pay for it. If they get in a car accident, hopefully they have the right insurance to cover them in case they need medical care, or to fix their car, or if the person that hit them doesn't have coverage. They want to know that it works for them. There is a huge opportunity here because people don't know anything about insurance. That gives you the opportunity to provide value to them. Educate them. Teach them. This is the beauty of it.

You can pull them to the direction that they need to go. If you were to teach somebody about insurance, a new salesperson, for example, you would teach them about all the different types of insurance products that are out there. More importantly, you would teach them why they need the insurance. You'd teach them what those different insurance policies are and what they would actually cover. Does it just cover an auto crash, or does it cover if the other person involved is uninsured? Does it cover this type of injury and not that type of injury?

What you can do in providing value is two-fold. One is on the upfront. It's when you're talking to a client. People want to get the cheapest policy possible, but is that always the best thing for them? Julie, may I ask you, is the cheapest policy always best for them?

No, it's not.

Yeah, I didn't think it would be. I wouldn't call it upsell because you're not really upselling it. Upsell has a bad connotation to it. You're value selling to them stuff that they actually need. If you care about your clients, you provide them products that they actually need. In your case, insurance coverage that they actually need, and they're going to thank you for it. They're not going to feel that they're being swindled out of it.

That's just for the upfront. Then, something that I think would be huge for your business, would be to do, maybe every six months, a six-month insurance review. It's as simple as this.

You call up each client every six months from the anniversary date of their policy, which is probably a great time because I'm guessing a lot of policies, depending what state you're in, renew every six months. Auto policies where I'm from renew in that time period. You can talk to your clients and say, "Hey, I currently see that you have this coverage, and it's doing well for you. How are you feeling about this coverage?" Make sure to let them know that everything is good. You can see if there are any new discounts that have come out that they may qualify for. You can see if they have any new vehicles. You want to make sure that you're all covered. "Any new vehicle purchases, any motorcycles? Did you buy an ATV? Oh, did you get any jewelry?" to kind of probe into their life a little bit, but providing value to them, making sure that they're fully covered.

As you do that, you may find out, "Oh, yeah, my wife just got pregnant." Boom. You found out that his wife is pregnant, and they may need to discuss life insurance. The benefit of this that you're providing value to them, but you also are going to be able to get hooked into them, deeper into their lives. Now that you know you'll be able to discuss a life insurance policy, then you ask about a boater's policy or another type of policy. The more of their life that you cover, the less likely that they are going to leave you. Not only are you going to keep those renewals going on, and on, and on, but those renewals are going to be bigger because you're getting in deeper into their lives.

I would also do this when you get their initial policy. I would let them know, "Hey, I'm setting up a time six months from now." Write in your calendar, if you use Outlook or Gmail. Say, "Every six months I call my clients, just to review policies with them, make sure they're getting the best possible price, and that the coverage they're getting is the right coverage. If we find out in six months that this is too much, then we'll look to take your coverage down a little bit. If we see that your coverage is not enough, we'll look to take this up a little bit." It's really important that you let them know that you're also going to look to see if you can save them money every six months. Again, you said it's more important to have the renewals than it is to get the highest dollar amount policy because if they leave, you'll never get those renewals.

Does that make sense? You can see how that's bringing value to the client?

Yeah, DJ, that makes a lot of sense, and I know my clients would love to know that I'm making sure they're always getting the right coverage and great pricing. It's so simple actually.

Julie, you're right. It is so simple but people never follow-up with their past clients. They're the easiest people to sell more to, keep happy, and they're the ones that are going to bring in referrals.

If, for instance, you're doing your six-month review with these people, you ask them, "Hey, has this been beneficial for you? How are you liking the coverage?"

They say, "Oh, it's been great, Julie, we love everything that you do."

"Great, can you do me a huge favor? Can you give me the name of three of your friends, that you think that are just like you, that would be a great fit for my company? I would really love to work with more people like you."

"Yeah, Julie, we'd be more than happy to do that."

"Wonderful. What are their names and their phone numbers?" They give it to you. Boom, then you just got yourself three new leads. Not only are you going to be getting more of their coverages, you're going to keep them for longer, and when you do an every six-month review you're going to be able to get more referrals. You can ask them for these referrals with confidence because you're providing tremendous value. A reason a lot of salespeople are afraid to ask for referrals is because they provided no value to their clients. Julie, you finding this helpful?

Yes, DJ, this is really helpful, and it's actually pretty easy. This is going to help out tremendously!

Hey, Julie, I'm glad you said it's easy. I don't want any of this to be complicated. The sales industry is not complicated. It's actually really, really easy. The principle, bringing massive value to people, your clients, or your referral sources, is where it's at. You can see it as your business grows. You need to bring more value. As you bring value, your business grows, grows, and grows. It's the principle of reaping and sowing.

All right, let's see who's next.

Chapter 12

Now we've got Jeff Thompson. Jeff, raise your hand so that the usher can come track you down and hand you the microphone. Jeff, how are you doing today?

DJ, I'm doing fanfreakintastic! How are you?

First, I love your enthusiasm! As for me, I'm loving life because I'm doing what I love. I am talking with you guys about business, about sales, about helping people. Life is good. Jeff, tell us a little bit. What is it you do for a living?

DJ, I am an online marketer. Specifically, I generate sales leads for companies in various different industries.

Very cool, Jeff. What are different ways that you do that right now?

The big one for me is really Facebook campaigns. I do some paid traffic like on Google and such, but the biggest thing that I use is Facebook.

Alright, Jeff, let me ask you, what is it that you're looking to get into, or how can I help you help grow your business?

For me right now, I've got a pretty good niche going on with helping generate leads for real estate and lenders. It's a pretty big opportunity to market. But it's a market that's flooded with different people, trying to get the business for realtors, for lenders. It seems that there's always people saying they can get leads for them, and they're always like a ping-pong ball, just bouncing back and forth, getting knocked around. It's hard to keep people, even if you are providing good leads, because they hear somebody that says they can do it cheaper, so they go. Then they can't do it cheaper, the leads are crap, and then they come back me. It's just a mess. I'd like to see if I can branch into some other markets

Sorry to laugh, Jeff, but I totally get it, and I know what you're talking about. Trying to work with lenders and Realtors, it's like herding sheep at times. We can be finicky people, all over the board. You're right, there's people always coming after us to provide leads in business, and claim to generate better leads. You're also right, most of them are crap. I wish more people would stick with the same person that provides them some solid leads, even if the leads cost a bit more money. If they're better quality leads, obviously that makes more sense, but that's neither here nor there. You said you were trying to break in other markets. What kind of markets were you thinking about getting into?

Well, one of the things I'd like to do is get into the trades. My father, who's a tradesman, is a blue-collar guy. It sounds like you said your family is from blue-collar. I'd just like to work with them and help people in those industries, specifically, to grow more. There are roofing, window and siding contractors. There's even some remodeling. There's some good-sized margins in there, and I find these people do fantastic work. They're just having trouble generating new business and new leads. They have roller coaster months, where they are doing really good a couple of months, but then they don't have the leads coming in, and then they're slow. They're up and they're down. Their skill is in the work they do. They're not marketers and whenever they hire someone to market for them they get terrible results.

Jeff, that's funny that you talk about the roller coaster months, we could talk forever on that. What are the struggles you have getting into this? Do you have the proof that you could generate great leads, and that they're making money for the Realtors and the lenders? What struggles are you having getting in with these companies? Are you not able to speak to the right people, or what's the deal?

Really, I can speak to the right people, but it's something that they've never done before or the people they hired to helped did a poor job. They are hesitant to spend the money to pay me to generate these new kinds of leads, and pay for the ad and all of that. It's a difficult proposition for them to take that risk, pull out money from

their marketing budget, and pay me to generate
these leads.

Jeff, if I understand, you have the right people you can target, whether it's roofers, siding, windows. You have been able to get in and have conversations with them, but they're having difficulty pulling the trigger due to cost. Is that right?

Yeah, DJ, that's exactly right.

Let me ask you, Jeff, do you believe in what you do? Are you good at what you do? You know that you can generate them leads that will turn into sales?

Yeah, of course I do. I'm good at what I do, and I know I can generate them business. Like I said, they don't want to pay me for the ad spend. Or they'll pay the ad spend, but they're not sure about my fees. I charge a few grand a month to do it, and then a per-lead basis.

Let me ask you then, what would you think about offering them something like this? They're afraid of their spending costs, because it might not work, and I totally get that. Again, you want to look to bring value to them. What is something that you can do that would eliminate that fear as much as possible? What about if you were to go with this value proposition, and say, "Hey, Mr. Roofer, I understand that you're interested in trying this out. You believe in what I can do for you, but you're a little nervous of the cost, of what it would be to pay me to do it, the ad spend and then the per lead cost that it would be for you. But what if I could eliminate almost all of those costs for you and you don't pay me a penny unless you get sales?"

Let's say that you commit to spend $500 a month, or $1,000 on ad spend. Jeff, you know what kind of ad spend they would need so tweak as necessary. You commit to that. Then I will do all of the work. I will spend all of the hours creating the ads, follow up campaigns, email drips, sales letters, etc. And if these leads don't turn into sales, I get paid zilch, however, if a lead does convert into a sale, I get paid a percent of that sale. This way your risk is greatly minimized while your reward is greatly maximized. It also gives me greater incentive for you to be successful, Mr Roofer."

Now Jeff, do you think that is something they would like? Is that something they would do, they would pay you on closed business versus paying you on creating ads that they don't know will work or not?

Yeah, they would probably love that.

Let me ask you, Jeff, do you think you could make more money by just being paid a flat fee to create some ads, and create some leads for them? Or do you think you could make more money getting a percentage of the gross sales in each deal?

You know, I probably could make a lot more money if I did it that way.

Does that sound like a win for you, Jeff, if you can make more money off of each of these clients?

Yeah, of course it is.

More importantly, does it sound like a win for those potential clients? That they could eliminate their concern of paying you to generate leads that don't work? But instead pay you *only* when they're successful? Do you think they would do that?

Absolutely, they would do that.

Think they'd love that?

Absolutely, they would love it!

You're generating the leads, they close the leads, and you get paid on it. Boom, everybody wins. You see how I'm thinking outside the box a little bit, and how to set up your business relationship a little differently? Eliminate the friction, eliminate the reasons that they can say no, and just create more opportunities for them to say yes. You can see, as they do that, their business is going to grow because you know that the leads that you provide are rock solid. Their business will grow. As their business grows, because you set up a deal with them that you get a percentage of their gross sales from the deals that you help close, you will make more money. It's a huge win. There's no risk for anybody here. The only risk is for you, because you don't get paid anything, if you generate leads that don't sell. It's just like a salesperson. If I don't sell, I don't close, I don't make deals, I don't get paid. Same thing with you. If you generate leads that don't turn into deals, you don't get paid. That can be scary, but you can also see how there's so much more upswing potential. Does that make sense, Jeff?

Yeah, it makes perfect sense.

Is that something you can do? Do you think that's something you can start implementing in your business, so it will create value for your clients and create value for you?

Yes, absolutely.

I know it's only been a few minutes, but have you found that helpful and valuable?

Absolutely, DJ. That makes so much more sense when you say it that way.

I tell you, Jeff, it's not like I have all this stuff figured out. It's just seeing your business from a different angle, and seeing opportunity you may have never seen.

Thanks, everybody. It looks like I've got time for one more person, and just so you know,

after this one, we'll talk about my Mastermind
where I'll personally help you grow your
business with the principles I'm talking with you
today. Okay, we've got one more, so who's
going to be the last lucky one?

Chapter 13

Last, but certainly not least, Gina Thompson. Gina, raise your hand so the ushers can come to you. All right, Gina, how are you doing today?

I'm doing wonderful. I'm so happy that you called my name. It's the last one. I heard you call my name and got pretty damned excited. Thank you. I'm looking forward to hearing what you have to say.

It's my pleasure, Gina. I see from your business card that you are a mortgage lender. Mortgage lenders representing in the house, I see. Gina, you obviously know that's what I do for a living. I'm a mortgage lender, or at least that's my main career. I've talked a little bit about my path. Let me ask. How are things for you? Where are your struggles? What can I help you with today?

Well, DJ, I've been doing this for quite a while now. I've been a lender now for a little over 20 years. Actually, it'll be 24 years. This is my 24th year. I do well. I make over six figures but not much more year in and year out. I've kind of hit that glass ceiling that you and some of the other people talked about. I'm finding that no matter what I do, I just don't get more than what I getting. I'm happy with it, but I want to save a little bit more for my retirement. I know, with my past history and my client base, all my clients say they love me and all that stuff, but I could be doing more.

That's awesome, Gina. Thanks for sharing and being so honest. Let me ask you to clarify, would you like to talk more about your Realtor relationships, or would you like to talk more about your relationships with your past clients, or new buyers that are coming in? What are you wanting to talk about?

Well, I'd like to talk about all of them, but if I have to pick one, I'd really like if we could talk about how to convert more of the clients that get referred in to me, whether they're referred in by past customers, or from a Realtor, or from a marketing thing that I do. What are ways that I can bring value to those people, so I can convert a higher percentage of them? I know if I do that, obviously, I will make more money that way.

To me, Gina, for each of those you'd have to have a slightly different value equation or a different value that you would bring to each of those situations. Let's talk about these in general. Are these people looking to buy houses, or are these people looking for refinances? It's very important, because you'll notice as time goes on, as I talk about these sorts of things, you really need to segment as much as possible who you're talking to. These are people that are referred in to you. Are they buyers, or are they people looking to refinance?

Let's say they're buyers.

OK, they're buyers. I can continue to refine that list even more, like first-time buyers, repeat buyers, big houses, small houses, all those things, but let's just talk about all of them right now, as buyers in general. What's one thing that they all need, whether they know it or not? What is one thing they all need to make sure that the process goes as smoothly as possible for them?

Well, DJ, to make it go smoothly they really need to know what the new laws are, what the mortgage industry is like, and all the things they will need, including paperwork they need to have. They just really need to know more about how the mortgage process works.

Gina, bingo. That's exactly it. They need to know those things. The problem is, as lenders, we expect them to know. We tell them a little bit of information, and we don't explain it enough or tell them why they need to know those things and why they're important. You know, as a part of the mortgage industry, we have to collect all types of information from them. We need to have their bank statements. I know from bank statements you need to have not just the first page of numbers, but you need to have all pages of bank statements, even if the fifth page is not relevant. You need to have their tax returns with all of their schedules. You need their pay stubs. You need all of these things.

One way to position yourself with people is to be a better educator for them, to educate them through every step of the process and to help them understand the different loan programs. Not just giving them facts, but providing them with pros and cons, and showing how that will fit into their lives.

When I talk to my clients, I really talk to them. We need to figure out the best financial move for them, and for their family. We need to look at their specific situation, whether they're planning on making this their forever home or this is going to be a house they plan on staying in for a couple years and then either sell it and move up or keep it and rent it out. The more questions you ask, the deeper you can go into their lives. Just like we were talking about with the insurance, the deeper you can go into it with them, the stronger of a bond you'll form with them, and the more likely they'll stay with you.

Now let me share something that's pretty cool. I know a lot of times people say, "Well, that's going to take a long time. How am I supposed to do that with every client and still grow my business?" Let me tell you something I do that's super simple, that I learned from a mentor of mine. I have tons of videos that people see. Whether it's through an online marketing campaign I'm doing, through a referral from a Realtor that comes in, or it's a past client, they see videos of me. They see this different information before they ever talk with me that educates them, and teaches them things they need to know. That way, by the time they get to me, they're basically ready to hit the ground running. Obviously, I still talk with them, but the point is that these people are already pre-sold on working with me.

Of the people that are referred in to me, whether it's from online marketing, or a past client referred them to me, or it's a Realtor referral, if they are able to get a mortgage, over 90% of the time they are sold on doing business with me before I talk with them. It's because of the way that I educate them up front on the things they need to know.

There are tons of information in the world through the Internet that anyone can look up on their cell phone. You can search mortgage and find a million things about mortgages. It doesn't mean it's all right. It doesn't mean it's all relevant. Somebody might pull up an article from 2008. Do you think that's relevant today? Is it going to be relevant in 5 years? Heck, no. That's what we need to do. We need to set the expectations up front, telling people what they need to know and why they need to know it. You need to change your idea of what your position is and become a teacher, an educator. That can be done without being condescending, or talking down to them. Make sure they know they can ask you any kind of question. They can email you. They can call you. No matter what, they can come to you. Make sure you let them know. Tell them you want them to come to you with any questions they have. You want to be the person that they go to when they have a mortgage question. If they hear something on the radio and they want to know about it, have them call you. If they see some crazy thing on the Internet, have them call you. You want them going to you for the information, not going to their friends, not going to that article that they read, not listening to that crazy person on the radio saying that they have zero percent interest rates, or whatever stupid things people use to hook clients. You want to be the trusted source of information. That is value that you can bring to the table, not just information, but education. If you are the person that they come to and get the right information, and get educated, they will never leave you. Best of all, they will tell everybody about you, because whether it's their first house or it's their last house, a basic starter home or a big multi-million dollar estate on the lake, if you can bring them value with solid education, they will be loyal to you forever.

That way, when you can call them down the road and do a mortgage review with them every 6 months, every 12 months or whatever it is, it will be easy to ask for referrals. It will be easy to ask for more business, see if they're looking into investment properties or see if they have any interest in refinancing. You will build a bond. When you provide that value to them up front, you've created yourself a client for life. Clients for life will be worth tens of thousands of dollars to you, not just in their own business but in the business they refer to you.

Well, I'm out of breath on that one a little bit. You can tell I'm a little bit passionate about that!

Gina, does that make sense, on how it's so important to bring value in that regard to clients that come in? It's not just with mortgages. It's any sort of service industry. Say you're a chiropractor or whatever, you're going to be sending out monthly emails, or newsletters, or mailers about health and how to stay healthier, such as tips on, "Oh, this new vitamin is out. What's the truth about this vitamin or this pill?" You can be the person they go to for trusted information. If you're that person they come to for information, you're going to be the person they come to when they need your services. It doesn't matter what the service is, whether it's mortgages, insurance, accounting, selling computer systems, or selling leads. No matter what it is, what product or service you sell, if you can be the person that they seek out, the person that they go to for information, you will have them as a client. It's easy. It's not selling at that point. It's just educating. Education sells. Why? It's because you don't need to close them, because you're providing them valuable information they need to know. Then they can make the right choice. Since you are the person that provided them with the right information, to them you are the right choice to do business with.

Gina, was that helpful? Was that a lot?

Yeah, DJ, that was helpful, and it was a lot, but I totally see what you say. I've kind of become just an order-taker. "Here's my interest rate. Here are my costs." Instead, I'd be educating my clients and getting to know their situation, not having the boxed approach for every single person, but really finding a custom solution for them. I can totally see how that's going to benefit them, not just for today, but for the rest of their lives.

You've got that right, Gina. That's exactly right. Well, everybody, I think we talked to five people. I'd like to do more, but my time is running down, so I want to transition this into a close.

Chapter 14

Now I'm wrapping things up. This is typically the part of a presentation where the person hosting or that's given the speech, talk whatever you want to call it, is trying to strong-arm you, trying to persuade you to get into their program, sign up for this service, join their coaching program. They pull out whatever techniques that they have to try to show how clever they are to convince you. That's not my style, as you could tell. My style is to bring massive value to people's businesses, because I know as they're successful, I'll be more successful. That's how I view my coaching program, my Mastermind. I don't have a special name for it but, basically, it's a business growth program where we're going to break the glass ceiling and take your businesses to new heights.

Let me talk about that, what you all get with it. It's pretty simple. Keep things simple but with lots of value. First and foremost, twice a month, we will have a two-hour call, and the calls will be recorded in case you cannot make it. Two things will be happening on these calls. First thing, each month we'll focus on a particular topic that is all about growing your business. For example, one of the months we'll be focusing on creating an offer that is so irresistible that you'll want to buy it for yourself. While another month we'll focus on building you a team or staff to support your current business and future growth. The topics that are covered each month are strategically set up so you can build in a healthy progression. A second thing that happens on each of these calls is an open time to discuss any struggle you're currently having and strategies to overcome them, and these struggles do not need to relate to the monthly topic. On these calls will also be the other members of the Mastermind. The reason why we do this as a group call is because we can learn things from one another. I believe in the principle of iron sharpening iron. There may be someone that's in a completely unrelated

industry than yours, but you could still learn
principles from the things that they're doing and
what they're doing in their business that's
working well for them. You can implement it to
your business.

In addition to that, you'll have direct access
to me, whether you want to email me, text me,
or Facebook message me, or whatever it is. I'm
here to help your business.

Another great thing as part of this is, once a
month I'll be doing a webinar for everybody in
the group, and it won't just be me talking. I will
have a guest on the webinar, somebody that's a
legend in their particular industry that will help
propel your business more quickly. They may be
Facebook ad experts, automation experts, team
building pros, paid traffic. You name it, there
will be someone that covers it. The webinars
with those people alone are well worth the cost
of this Mastermind, because getting these people
together on your own would cost you several
thousands of dollars just for an hour of their
time. Yet, they're going to be doing it for you,

because you're a part of this exclusive Mastermind.

The other part of what you get with all of this is somebody, me, to work alongside you, to encourage you, help you grow and stay focused on the goals that you have set; to help you implement the plans of creating massive value to your clients and to your referral partners. Again, as we talked about, you reap what you sow.

Today, you're going to start taking the steps of sowing massive seeds of value into your business and to the people you work with in your business. How much does this cost? It's a 12-month Mastermind that's set up to build off of each month, and it's $1,500 a month. However, you won't have to sign a long-term contract. It's month-to-month because if you don't find value in it, you don't have to continue with it.

Now let me ask you, is $1,500 per month worth the investment if it increased your business just 25%? What about 50%? 100%? 1,000%? What we'll be going over and implementing each month will do that for your business.

How do you sign up? First, you don't sign up. You apply because not everyone will be accepted. But, to apply, go to my website, www.evolutionofasalesman.org. That's www.evolutionofasalesman.org. There's a form that you fill out so I get to know a little bit more about you and get a little more in depth about your business so I can see where things are, and what your goals and aspirations are. Then, there's going to be an interview, a one-on-one interview directly with me. At that time, we're going to go over what I call the three Cs.

This is very important to me, and we cannot have a relationship if all three Cs aren't met. They're not in any specific order, and these are the same principles I use when I hire people. The first C is for competency. What is competency? This relates to how well you know your profession. Can you teach and educate others about your business? If you're not competent in what you do, it doesn't matter how much value you bring. You're not going to be successful. You're going to hit a certain level and stop growing. You need to be competent in your business. Also, I don't want to help you just explode your business before you're competent in it, because you'll never be able to handle it.

Two is your character. Are you the kind of person that I would trust? Are you the kind of person that I would like to do business with? Are you the kind of person that I would like to associate with? Because I'd be working with you, my name is directly tied with you. If I don't think that you're a person of character, I will not do business with you. I don't care how much you would pay me.

Third is something a lot of people don't think about, but I think it's really important. Chemistry. You might be completely competent and brilliant. You might have great character, but we just don't match. We don't click. We butt heads too much, or our styles just don't mix. We can maybe make things work but life's too short, and I'd rather work with people that I mesh with pretty well, especially on something as important as this.

There you have it. That's what I have to offer you. $1,500 per month. You get the two-hour call twice a month. You have direct access to me. You have the once a month webinar where I bring fantastic guests on, and you're going to have the accountability to keep you on track.

Ladies and gentlemen, I want to again, thank you for your time. That's what I have to offer you. I hope I brought massive value to your business. I hope it gets you thinking about how you can change things in your business to help other people become more successful, whether it's with your services or the products you have to offer. Start thinking more about other people and how they can hit the goals that they have, and the dreams that they have. The more people you help accomplish their dreams and goals, the bigger the dreams you yourself will have and obtain. Thank you.

To learn more about DJ's Mastermind, read his blog posts, check out some videos, and/or get some free content to help grow your business, check out his website:

www.EvolutionOfASalesman.org

Don't forget to like the Facebook page and join the Facebook group

www.facebook.com/EvolutionOfASalesman